FROM THE
INSIDE / OUT

What is
Manifesting?

HENRY W. WRIGHT

Be In Health™

4178 Crest Highway
Thomaston, Georgia 30286
(800) 453-5775

www.beinhealth.com

Disclaimer

This ministry does not seek to be in conflict with any medical or psychiatric practices nor do we seek to be in conflict with any church and its religious doctrines, beliefs or practices. We are not a part of medicine or psychology, yet we work to make them more effective, rather than working against them. We believe many human problems are fundamentally spiritual with associated physiological and psychological manifestations. This information is intended for your general knowledge only. Information is presented only to give insight into disease, its problems and its possible solutions in the area of disease eradication and/or prevention. It is not a substitute for medical advice or treatment for specific medical conditions or disorders. You should seek prompt medical care for any specific health issues. Treatment modalities around your specific health issues are between you and your physician.

As pastors, ministers, and individuals of this ministry, we are not responsible for a person's disease, nor are we responsible for his/her healing. All we can do is share what we see about a problem. We are not professionals; we are not healers. We are only ministers ministering the Scriptures, and what they say about this subject, along with what the medical and scientific communities have also observed in line with this insight. There is no guarantee that any person will be healed or any disease be prevented. The fruits of this teaching will come forth out of the relationship between the person and God based on these insights given and applied. This ministry is patterned after the following scriptures: 2 Corinthians 5:18-20; 1 Corinthians 12; Ephesians 4; Mark 16:15-20.

ISBN   0-9786255-2-8
EAN   978-0-9786255-2-8

Copyright Notice

Preface

This booklet was developed from a live teaching to an audience and has been kept in a conversational format. It is designed to reach a personal level with the reader rather than present a structured, theological presentation.

Many times the reader will feel that Pastor Henry is talking directly to him/her. The frequent use of the pronoun *you* is meant to penetrate the human heart for conviction, not for accusation.

The purpose of this booklet is self-examination.

But the fruit of the Spirit is love, joy, peace, longsuffering, gentleness, goodness, faith, meekness, temperance:

against such there is no law.

GALATIANS 5:22-23

Table of Contents

PRACTICE MAKES PERFECT.

PRACTICE MANIFESTING the fruit of the Spirit.

Introduction

Paul effectively said in the Scriptures that we should each take up our own cross daily.

> **23And he said to *them* all, If any *man* will come after me, let him deny himself, and take up his cross daily, and follow me.**   Luke 9:23

We Christians always think of the cross as a positive thing, but the cross represents the curse. It represents those things that are the opposite of what God saw to be in our lives before the foundation of the world. So when Paul said every man should pick up his own cross, he did not mean go to church, carry a Bible, or sing a song. He meant we should deal with our stuff*.

"What you will not deal with" will deal with you.

What you do not defeat in your life will defeat you. We could get into a long story about every person's journey. You might say, "Well, I just don't know about Suzie". Well, she is on her journey, not yours.

Mark 9 is graphic and says,

> **47And if thine eye offend thee, pluck it out: it is better for thee to enter into the kingdom of God with one eye, than having two eyes to be cast into hell fire:**   Mark 9:47

---

* Refer to Be in Health™ Idioms.

The Spirit of God does not want you to be casual. God wants to preserve you, and it's time to practice being preserved.

The Bible says,

³¹For if we would judge ourselves, we should not be judged.
1 Corinthians 11:31

If you have a hand that takes you where you do not need to go, it is best that you cut that hand off and go into heaven with one hand, rather than having two hands and go into hell fire.

⁴³And if thy hand offend thee, cut it off: it is better for thee to enter into life maimed, than having two hands to go into hell, into the fire that never shall be quenched: ⁴⁴Where their worm dieth not, and the fire is not quenched.
Mark 9:43-44

"Where their worm dieth not" is a direct quote from Isaiah 66, talking about the essence of life.

²⁴And they shall go forth, and look upon the carcasses of the men that have transgressed against me: for their worm shall not die, neither shall their fire be quenched; and they shall be an abhorring unto all flesh. Isaiah 66:24

In hell, you are conscious and still have memory. In hell, you become just like an evil spirit, having every urge of evil and no way to fulfill it, having every urge of sin and no physical body with which to fulfill it. An evil spirit is disembodied, with every urge of its fallen being and no way to express it; for example, having lust, yet no one to lust with because it needs a physical body to fulfill lust. Hell is having every tormented thought forever and no way to express it.

That is the state of devils. They need humans to fulfill themselves so that the human can join them in the same torment.

In Mark 9, the Bible talks about your eyes, your feet, and your hands: where your eyes take you, where your hands are placed, and where your feet walk. It says that it is better to deal with it and go into heaven missing a member than to end up in hell fire with both members still present.

Every one of us is called to a journey. Every one of us is called out of darkness to be light and salt.

It's time for us to be more light and more salt than we have been in the past. The Spirit of God is calling your families out of darkness. Jeremiah 3:14 says,

¹⁴Turn, O backsliding children, saith the LORD; for I am married unto you: and I will take you one of a city, and two of a family, and I will bring you to Zion: Jeremiah 3:14

It does not mean everyone in your cities will be saved. It does not mean everyone in your families will be saved. It means out of your cities and your families, God will call a people, and then out of that people, some will be chosen.

¹⁴For many are called, but few *are* chosen. Matthew 22:14

Not everyone who has heard the message will make it into eternity. Not everyone who has responded to the

3

message will be found faithful as an overcomer and stay true. The Bible is very clear; it says,

> [22]...He that endureth to the end shall be saved.
>
> Matthew 10:22

Many scriptures address the overcomers.

> [7]...To him that overcometh will I give to eat of the tree of life . . .
>
> Revelation 2:7

> [11]...He that overcometh shall not be hurt of the second death.
>
> Revelation 2:11

> [17]...To him that overcometh will I give to eat of the hidden manna...
>
> Revelation 2:17

> [26]...he that overcometh . . . to him will I give power over the nations:
>
> Revelation 2:26

> [5]...He that overcometh . . . I will not blot out his name out of the book of life...
>
> Revelation 3:5

> [12]...Him that overcometh will I make a pillar in the temple of my God...
>
> Revelation 3:12

I do not want to be morbid and lay a heavy one[*] on you, but the Spirit of God is working with your hearts in this teaching. Do not go into another year practicing more of the same.

It's time for a change, and if you are interested in change, find a good church where you can practice. I also ...want to be changed. There are things where my eyes, my hands and

---

[*] Refer to Be in Health™ Idioms.

my feet take me that are not of heaven. How many of you could say there are parts of your life where your eyes, your hands and your feet take you that may not be of heaven?

It's time for a change.

We are not practicing for eternity. No, eternity is here right now. If you are born again, you will never see death. On the other side of death, you will exist in a disembodied state. You cannot escape; you will just wake up on the other side, in the same peace or the same torment.

Whether you are saved or not saved, there is life after death.

I want to share a rather simple word study regarding who you are. I want to talk about ways to keep the enemy from plaguing you. I want to give you some keys about how to be more free next year rather than to stay in prison houses. Just because you are saved does not mean you are not in some type of prison house. There are many believers everywhere who are prisoners of Satan, who are held captive by Satan at his will.

You may say, "Well, I don't think a believer can be held captive by Satan at his will".

Then you don't know your Bible. You don't even have to read the Bible to look around and see believers bound by Satan. You don't even need a Bible to prove the point that many believers are not free. They are bound by many psychological and biological problems. Have you read 2 Timothy 2:24-26?

> 24And the servant of the Lord must not strive; but be gentle unto all men, apt to teach, patient, 25In meekness instructing those that oppose themselves; if God peradventure will give them repentance to the acknowledging of the truth; 26And that they may recover themselves out of the snare of the devil, who are taken captive by him at his will.
>
> 2 Timothy 2:24-26

These verses are addressed to believers who are being held captive by the devil.

I want to insert into your life some concepts, and some precepts. I don't want you to listen to me today and walk out of here saying, "Wasn't that good?" There is nothing good, except God. What I have to share with you today would possibly be a lamp unto your feet and a light unto your pathway, to give you some goals that reflect how God thinks, and how He would speak, and how He would act.

> 105Thy word *is* a lamp unto my feet, and a light unto my path.
>
> Psalms 119:105

How God thinks needs to be the work of the Holy Spirit, not only in our own lives, but also in our relationship with our wives and our husbands; in our relationships in our own families, with our children and grandchildren; in our relationships in our jobs and our businesses; and even in our relationships in the church body.

You need to know how God thinks.

How God thinks needs to be a work of the Holy Spirit in our lives not only here, but outside these gates of safety, in the midst of the world and among those around us who are not renewed spiritually. When you are subjected to their idiosyncrasies on a regular basis because they are unrenewed and unspiritual, you need to know how God thinks.

Then again, just because you are a Christian does not mean that you are renewed, and it does not mean you are spiritual. In fact, I have seen some sinners more righteous than saints. I have seen some husbands who are sinners love their wives, and I have seen Christian men beat their wives.

Don't be a sinning saint!
Don't be an unbelieving believer!

Being born again is no guarantee of your spirituality, and there is more to salvation than being born again and going to heaven. <u>Now</u> is the appointed time. <u>Now</u> is the day of salvation.

> ²For he saith, I have heard thee in a time accepted, and in the day of salvation have I succoured thee: behold, now *is* the accepted time; behold, now *is* the day of salvation.
> 2 Corinthians 6:2

Salvation is more than being born again. The question that I would lay on your hearts is this: Have you been converted since you believed?

Are you in the process of being converted since you believed?

We always equate conversion with being born again. That is a religious blindfold. You must be born again. Your

7

spirit must come alive to God, but it's no guarantee that you have been converted.

Acts 3:19 says,

> **¹⁹Repent ye therefore, and be converted, that your sins may be blotted out, when the times of refreshing shall come from the presence of the Lord.** Acts 3:19

I want the times of refreshing from the presence of the Lord to come to you more than it has ever come before. I want to give you some clues about how this can occur. If you will line up with how God thinks, what He says and what He would do, you're going to find that He, invisibly, will rebuke the devourer for your sake.

> **¹¹And I will rebuke the devourer for your sakes, and he shall not destroy the fruits of your ground; neither shall your vine cast her fruit before the time in the field, saith the LORD of hosts.** Malachi 3:11

You will never see it happening. You will never experience it, but you will experience the lack of problems.

There is a greater principle of not needing healing available to you, and it is found in 3 John 2.

> **²Beloved, I wish above all things that thou mayest prosper and be in health, even as thy soul prospereth.** 3 John 1:2

**A greater principle
than being healed and delivered
is to be in health!**

When Jesus began to teach, He did not teach about the gifts. In Matthew 5, in the Sermon on the Mount, He did not teach about eschatology. He did not teach about prophetic timeline, going to heaven, being born again, defeating the devil, spiritual warfare, and all the other things that we consider to be so very essential.

He began to teach about what we should look like as human beings. He began to show us what we should look like in creation according to the way He thinks.

> **5Blessed *are* the meek: for they shall inherit the earth. 7Blessed *are* the merciful: for they shall obtain mercy. 8Blessed *are* the pure in heart: for they shall see God. 9Blessed *are* the peacemakers: for they shall be called the children of God.**   Matthew 5:5, 7-9

You know all of these verses, but just because you know them doesn't mean you practice them. The church is filled with the knowledge of things that it does not practice. When you teach something, but do not practice it, then it becomes a stench and a vanity because you become a hearer rather than a doer of the Word. The Bible says,

> **22But be ye doers of the word, and not hearers only, deceiving your own selves.**   James 1:22

I want to take you on a study called *What Is Manifesting?* What is manifesting in your thoughts, your words and your deeds? What is best for mankind, or what is the worst for mankind? What is manifesting through you? The invisible things of God are to be clearly seen in the visible, through the church.

20For the invisible things of him from the creation of the world are clearly seen, being understood by the things that are made, even his eternal power and Godhead; so that they are without excuse: Romans 1:20

Is hell or heaven manifesting through you?

So the invisible things of the invisible God must be clearly seen in creation, in the visible. "What is manifesting" are things of the invisible world of the second heaven ruled by Satan or things of the invisible world of the third heaven ruled by the Father. One kingdom must manifest or the other must manifest. Every human is manifesting one kingdom or the other or half of one and half of the other.

Every single human is leavened, and every one in this building, including the man talking to you, has a certain amount of leaven. A little leaven will leaven the whole lump.

9A little leaven leaveneth the whole lump. Galatians 5:9

It is time to purge the leaven. Why? Because without purging it, the times of refreshing cannot come from the presence of the Lord. I want your lives to be filled with blessing. I want your lives to be filled with sanity. I want your lives to be filled with health. Why? Because that is what God has said in His Word about you.

Editor's Note: The booklet on *Communion* is recommended for instruction of how to deal with the leaven in other people.

10

The Works of the Flesh

I want to take you to Galatians 5. Galatians teaches against legalism, but if you receive it with a wrong spirit, it can become a great teaching on legalism. If you receive this with a right spirit, you will call it love. Galatians 5:19-21 says,

> **19Now the works of the flesh are manifest, which are *these*; Adultery, fornication, uncleanness, lasciviousness, 20Idolatry, witchcraft, hatred, variance, emulations, wrath, strife, seditions, heresies, 21Envyings, murders, drunkenness, revellings, and such like: of the which I tell you before, as I have also told *you* in time past, that they which do such things shall not inherit the kingdom of God.** Galatians 5:19-21

That word "flesh" means satanic beings.

Editor's Note: Refer to teaching on Separation for more information on "sin as a being".

"Flesh," "carnal nature," and "old man" all mean a kingdom, disembodied, as found in Ephesians 6 by its characteristics. Our battle, our war, is not with flesh and blood.

> **12For we wrestle not against flesh and blood, but against principalities, against powers, against the rulers of the darkness of this world, against spiritual wickedness in high *places*.** Ephesians 6:12

Our war is not with ourselves or others, but with disembodied beings who, by their fallen nature, want to overthrow us in God's plan. So this kingdom wants to manifest, and it wants to manifest through humans. What

11

kind of things want to manifest through humans? The invisible things of that other god, Satan, who is called the god of mankind and the god of this world.

⁴In whom the god of this world hath blinded the minds of them which believe not, lest the light of the glorious gospel of Christ, who is the image of God, should shine unto them.
2 Corinthians 4:4

That kingdom wants to manifest through humans. Without humans, it cannot manifest, nor can it be seen. Did you ever see someone who was angry? How could you tell? Anger was manifesting. How could you tell? Because you observed the manifestation. You observed it because...

You watched invisible things manifesting in the visible.

That was the flesh manifesting. Have you ever seen someone that was full of fear? How could you tell? You could see it. Have you ever been around a bitter person? How did you know? You could see it manifesting. Have you ever been around someone that had sexual lust? How could you tell? When they came around you, you began to feel icky*. They were not interested in love. They were interested only in taking. That was the manifestation.

Paul is saying "the works of the flesh". "Works" means there is something happening. It is happening in humans, but it has its origin in something called "the flesh," which is non-human. The word "flesh" can mean your human body or the chicken you had for dinner yesterday, but in Scripture it

---

* Refer to Be in Health™ Idioms.

12

means the carnal nature, the old man, the body of sin by its fallen nature, which is a disembodied, intelligent kingdom as described in Ephesians 6.

Let's examine the works of the flesh.

Adultery

Adultery is having a sexual relationship with a person when you are married to someone else.

Fornication

Fornication is having a sexual relationship with someone, and you are not married. Having a sexual relationship with yourself (masturbation) is fornication unless you are married; then it is adultery.

If you are having sexual relationships with animals, that is bestiality. It has not been too many months ago that we had an individual who came to the earnest section and confessed, as a believer, to this sin.

Editor's Note: The earnest section is where people go during a worship service at Pleasant Valley Church to accept Christ as their Savior or to confess sin.

Do you think we ever blinked an eye about that? Bestiality is no greater sin than strife, but we categorize certain types of sin as acceptable, and other ones as evil. All sin is unrighteousness.

Uncleanness and Lasciviousness

Uncleanness and lasciviousness includes molestation, rape and other unclean acts for personal satisfaction and gratification.

IdolATRY

Idolatry is commonly thought of as having other gods. Stubbornness is also idolatry.

> [33]For rebellion *is as* the sin of witchcraft, and stubbornness *is as* iniquity and idolatry. Because thou hast rejected the word of the LORD, he hath also rejected thee from *being* king.
> 1 Samuel 15:23

When you know to do the truth, but do not do it, you are in idolatry of yourself because you have set yourself and what you think as higher than the thoughts of the living God who has spoken. When you overthrow and reject what God has said, after you have known the truth, then you are in self-idolatry.

When you know to do the truth, but do not do it, you have set yourself as a god against the true and living God.

WiTchcRAfT

This "witchcraft" is not the witchcraft of 1 Samuel 15. If we did the word study, we would find it means pharmaceutical drugs: FDA approved, properly prescribed and administered pharmaceutical drugs. That word "witchcraft," in the Greek, is *pharmakeia,* pharmacist, drug store, drugs, and legal drugs.

Editor's Note: The Greek word for witchcraft is *Strong's #5331, pharmakeia,* which means medication (pharmacy) or (by extension) magic (literal or figurative) and is translated sorcery or witchcraft in the King James Version. Be In Health™ is not opposed to doctors or medicine, but it is opposed to people taking a pill in order to bypass their spiritual issues.

Hatred

Hatred is rooted in bitterness. Unforgiveness, resentment, retaliation, rage and anger, violence and murder all have their roots in keeping a record of wrongs against God, others and yourself, and all are areas of hatred. There are those who hate God. There are those who hate others, and there are those who hate themselves. Hatred can be summed up in this one statement: "One of us has to go and it isn't me!"

Variance, Emulations

Variance and emulations. When you compare yourself to others, you may start to emulate the people you envy.

Editor's Note: The Greek word for variance is *Strong's #2054.* It means a quarrel or wrangling and is translated contention, debate, strife or variance.

Wrath, Strife

Wrath and strife. If you want everything that is evil to manifest, get into strife. We have spiritualized strife so that we don't hate sin anymore.

Editor's Note: Do you really hate sin? The first answer, of course, should be that you totally hate sin, but because you are still entangled with sin within you, you cannot give that as a right answer. The enemy will come to accuse you and say you like sin, so the answer should be, "I want to hate sin". Our prayer should be: I want to hate sin, so clean my cup and do whatever it takes to make me want to hate sin, like you hate sin. (exhortation by Pastor Donna on perfect hatred of sin)

The Bible says,

> **16For where envying and strife is, there is confusion and every evil work.**   James 3:16

Everything evil will manifest when there is strife.

Strife opens the door.

We have made adultery and fornication unpardonable sins, but strife is a national pastime, especially in churches and families.

Seditions

Seditions cause church splits, wars, anarchies, mutiny, and division in churches and families. It's a Luciferian, anti-Christ spirit. Seditions include uprisings that are against authority, touching God's anointed.

Heresies

Heresies are doctrines of devils that do not agree with how God thinks, what He has said, or how He would say it.

Any statement that does not match how God thinks or what He has said or what He would say is heresy.

Envyings

Envyings. You love what someone else has, but you hate them because <u>they</u> have it, and <u>you</u> do not.

Murders

Murders. Murders can be with a weapon or with the tongue.

Drunkenness

Drunkenness means the use of alcohol or illegal drugs causing altered states of consciousness other than what
16

God ordained that your consciousness should be. It is usually done to avoid the pain. Witchcraft or *pharmakeia* refers to legal drugs.

Revellings

Revellings mean partying too much, and in this setting people are made victims. There is the damage done from coarse jesting, date rape, straight rape, molestation, victimization, and such like.

And Such Like

"And such like" means there is more, but this is enough to think about for now!

> [21]...and such like: of the which I tell you before, as I have also told *you* in time past, that they which do such things shall not inherit the kingdom of God.   Galatians 5:21

Those who do such things shall not inherit the kingdom of God.

Word Study on "Do"

I looked up that word "do" because when I read it the first time, I figured that no one would ever go to heaven. I saw just about every Christian I knew doing part of this somewhere, including the man talking to you.

I said, "God, this is a hard word".

He said, "Look up the word".

17

I looked up the word "do" in the Greek, and here is what it said (and I could breathe again). The word "do" in the Greek in Galatians 5 means "those that habitually practice," as opposed to "a single act".

Editor's Note: "Do" in Galatians 5:21 comes from *Strong's #4238*. It means to "practice," to perform repeatedly or habitually rather than referring to a *single* act.

There are two types of humans: those who fall and are convicted, and those who fall, but are not convicted.

Those who fall, but are not convicted, have hardened their hearts, and they habitually practice these types of things. This verse is talking about believers, not sinners, who are habitually practicing the things of the flesh, without conscience and without repentance. Those believers who "habitually" practice these things shall not inherit the kingdom of God.

I don't know what that does to eternal security, but that is what it says "shall not inherit the kingdom of God". Why? If you will not deal with your sin here, you will forever pervert every human when you rule in eternity. You will lead nations into perversion, as a king and a priest. God cannot trust you.

If God cannot trust you here, why would He trust you to rule in the millennium?

Will God have another Lucifer on his hands? If God gave you a planet of humans to rule over in righteousness, would you establish His kingdom or would you listen to them, and cause them to go into rebellion against the great and living God? Would you end up with a world filled with

18

whoremongers, perverts, murderers, and warring individuals filled with strife, murder, and debate? Did God call you out of darkness for this type of activity? Did God call you out of darkness to establish more of the same?

The Fruit of the Spirit

I want to bring you to my point. All of the above was to set the stage for this message. I want to talk about the next few verses in Galatians 5, "the fruit of the Spirit". That word "Spirit" should be capitalized in your Bibles. There are translators that have taken the capital "S" away, and they will try to teach you that this is the fruit of the human spirit. The Bible says,

> **⁹The heart is deceitful above all things, and desperately wicked: who can know it?**   Jeremiah 17:9

> **¹⁰As it is written, There is none righteous, no, not one:**
>   Romans 3:10

There is not one person on this earth who is sinless, and if you say you are, you have just committed your first sin (lying). The next few verses are not on the fruit of the human spirit. That capital "S" means the fruit of the Holy Spirit. There are nine fruit(s) of the Holy Spirit.

Editor's Note: Scripture lists "fruit" as singular.

These are not things that you put on your refrigerator and stare at once a week. These are nine characteristics of God's incredible nature that you should practice daily.

> **²²But the fruit of the Spirit is love, joy, peace, longsuffering, gentleness, goodness, faith, ²³Meekness, temperance: against such there is no law.**   Galatians 5:22-23

If you will allow the Holy Spirit to form these nine characteristics of God in you, then you cannot be defeated.

Now, I want you to listen very carefully because I am going to ask the Holy Spirit to allow me to impart to you a direction for your life. You may not walk in this fully, every single day, beginning today. Nor do I, or will I, walk in it perfectly every day, but I trust the Holy Spirit will come and bring you into a focus, so that you will grow into this. We want you to grow up into the full measure and full stature of a man or woman of God, rather than remain a child stumbling through life.

¹³Till we all come in the unity of the faith, and of the knowledge of the Son of God, unto a perfect man, unto the measure of the stature of the fulness of Christ:

Ephesians 4:13

So do not think that I am laying a legalistic hammer on you, nor am I trying to kill you with truth, because if I kill you with truth, I am just going to have to raise you from the dead and start over again. The precepts of God are true.

⁴God forbid: yea, let God be true, but every man a liar; as it is written, That thou mightest be justified in thy sayings, and mightest overcome when thou art judged. Romans 3:4

So any man that would not agree with this is a liar. That is a strong statement!

These nine attributes of the Holy Spirit are nine characteristics of your Father in heaven and of the Lord Jesus' incredible, impeccable nature. In fact, these are nine areas of the best that you and I as humans could ever look like. How many of you like being around someone who is friendly? How many of you like being around people who are unfriendly? How many of you like being around

21

troublemakers? How many of you like being around peacemakers? How many of you like being around people that make you victims?

You know this truth too well already. Now it is time to take it from knowledge into a practical, day-by-day application.

It is time to practice being righteous daily.

How many of you want to practice being righteous? I do not mean in a self-righteous way. I am talking about the practice of being righteous out of a pure heart.

Those who are able to handle strong meat, who think they are mature, are those who by reason of use have exercised their senses to discern both good and evil.

> **14But strong meat belongeth to them that are of full age, *even* those who by reason of use have their senses exercised to discern both good and evil.** Hebrews 5:14

Spiritual exercise is more profitable than physical exercise. You need to exercise your spirit and your soul and spend less attention on your body. You need to get into the spiritual and soul exercise of discerning good and evil. In fact, the Bible very bluntly says,

> **8For bodily exercise profiteth little...** 1 Timothy 4:8

Begin to practice heaven.

You need to begin to practice the invisible things of the living God. So what if you blow it every other time! You are going to learn to walk in righteousness by practicing. When

22

you fall back into the old ways, what are you going to do? Repent to God! If you offend someone else, what are you going to do with them? Repent to them! Repent to God! Forgive them, forgive yourself, get back up and begin to practice righteousness day by day, until it is first nature to you, and not second nature.

Righteousness can become first nature to you.

Your human nature is evil. God's nature is the best you could be. I want to give you nine attributes of God's nature that should be human nature and God's nature combined. Do not forget you were created in God's image, and this is part of His image.

I am going to take each one of the nine attributes and refer to the Greek word that was used by Paul. I am going to the *Strong's Concordance* and read the definition for all nine. Through these definitions, you will be able to understand what you should look like. Then I am going to give you a missing link of divine protection.

There is a missing link of divine protection.

How many of you would like to be immune to the works of the devil? How many of you would like to be immune to victimization by the devil? I am going to show you an area where you do not even have to worry about spiritual warfare because there will be none. I said there will be no spiritual warfare, because you have become invincible.

It is time to become invincible!

That doesn't mean there will be no temptation in that invincibility. Invincibility does not guarantee eternal avoidance of temptation, but how many of you would like to be a better winner in temptation instead of losing to temptation so many times? What you are trying to do, Church, is to be an overcomer in disobedience.

You cannot be an overcomer while in rebellion.

You are trying to be an overcomer, yet you are not a doer of the Word. You are trying to be an overcomer in knowledge only. Having knowledge is no guarantee you will win. The Bible says,

> [7]Ever learning, and never able to come to the knowledge of the truth.   2 Timothy 3:7

Knowledge is essential, but knowledge without wisdom is futile. Wisdom plus knowledge, without fruit, is vanity. I want wisdom, and I want knowledge, plus wisdom, to produce fruits of righteousness. Do not be afraid of righteousness. There are millions of people paying psychologists trying to create wisdom through psychological healing, trying to change bad memories, trying to change the dark parts of themselves, trying drugs and counsel, and trying to be a god to themselves. Yet through God, it was freely available to them all the time.

Love

Love gives before it receives. Love is #26 (agape) in the Greek section of *Strong's Concordance* and is from the root word #25 (agapao). Root words help you understand the meaning. The root word is "to love," indicating an action. I hope you understand that love <u>first</u> gives before it receives.

24

LOVE: G26 agapē   *ag-ah'-pay* From G25; *love*, that is, *affection* or *benevolence*; specifically (plural) a *love feast:* - (feast of) charity ([-ably]), dear, love.

ROOT WORD OF LOVE: G25 agapaō   *ag-ap-ah'-o* (*much*); to *love* (in a social or moral sense): -   [(be-love (-ed)].

Love first gives before it receives.

So we are talking about loving others whether or not they love you in return. We are talking about God's nature. For God so loved the world...

16**For God so loved the world, that he gave his only begotten Son, that whosoever believeth in him should not perish, but have everlasting life.**   John 3:16

Love is an action that reaches out, whether you feel like it or not.

Did God love the world because they were righteous or did He love the world in their unrighteousness? Did God love you because you first loved him? God loved you when you were dead in your trespasses and sins. So God reached out to you in love, not expecting anything in return.

This message is important because it is critical to everything that pertains to you: your families, your marriages, your lives, your job and everything around you. As far as I am concerned, there is no greater sermon that I could give than this one because this is the bottom line of your freedom. I am calling you to attention as a matter of record. It is time to reach out, whether you feel like it or not.

This has nothing to do with your feelings. This has to do with how God thinks and what He has said. Many of you are sitting in your chairs and your homes, waiting for someone to reach out to you before you reach out to them. Some of you are embittered, because you do not think anyone has contacted you from this church or proved they love you. It is time to get this defeated. It is time to stop being so selfish in thinking that you are in need of something.

It's time to stop being so selfish.

I did not get into ministry because I needed anything. I got into ministry because I cared. You would be surprised how much we fight for your lives by establishing a safe place, doctrinally and positionally, so that you may grow. I have decided to reach out. I have decided to love. I have a small vision; it is just global. I do not care whether people are communist, Islamic, Buddhist, or Christian. It doesn't make any difference to me. It is time to love, and the first object of the word love (from the root word) is an action, which is "to love". Now the actual word that is used by Paul is love and affection.

Someone told me one time, "Pastor, I love you, but I just don't like you". Well, you are going to have to like me. You have no option, and I am committed to liking you. I have no option, but what we are trying to do is form people in our own image, for our own expectations. You know how many marriages are in trouble because some mate is trying to form (mold) the other member into what they think they should look like?

Marriages are in trouble
because one mate is trying to form the other

26

into what they think their mate should look like!

My job is not to form my wife into what I think she should look like. Pastor Donna Wright, my job is to undergird you on behalf of God so that you can grow up into everything that you should be in Him, and it may not be what I had in mind. In fact, there are maybe 19 things I would instantly change in you, if I had my way, and I know you have 46 things you would instantly change in me.

Love means benevolence and affection.

You may say, "Well, I have to love you because I'm a Christian". You don't have to love me because you're a Christian; you love me because that is who you are. It has to do with being a son or a daughter of God. I am almost embarrassed these days to be called a Christian because we are the laughingstock of the world.

Am I a son of God? Are you a son or daughter of God? Then love ought to be who we are.

It has to be an affectionate love, not a religious love. "Well, I sure love you…" You know, we give each other those denominational hugs. I grew up in a denominational movement so let me show you one.

[Giving "Sally" a side-hug] "I sure love you". But don't let the one you hugged last Sunday become the object of your discussion in the weekly prayer meeting. Don't say, "I think we ought to pray for Sister Sally. I discern…"

An affectionate love, not a religious love, is the fruit of the Spirit. It should not be "I have to" love, or "it is my duty" to love. It should be an affection. Can I challenge you to begin to become more affectionate? I do not mean slurping* on each other.

Love has a plural meaning.
It is the union of "more than one" with others.

This is powerful! Let's read some more. **The word _agape_ has a plural meaning. Love is not singular.** Love is not a one-way street. The word "love," _agape,_ means a love feast. We should be as in tune with loving each other in a love feast as if we are sitting down before a good meal. We should feast on our relationships one with another and learn to cultivate them.

A lot of people come to Pleasant Valley and do not realize they are checking out this _agape._ We call them "sniffers*". They come to see if they like what we represent. So they come to sniff, and that is okay. That is part of their deciding whether or not you are loving.

You must be "sniffable". When people come around to sniff you, they are filled with fears and rejections, and they are filled with sin. Love them! Say, "Sniff me some more!"

It's a feast of love, and another word with _agape_ is the word "dear".

(To Pastor Donna) "I love you, dear".

How many of you use the word "dear"? It means you love that person when you call them "dear". Love, as a work of

---

* Refer to Be in Health™ Idioms.

28

the Holy Spirit, ought to be first nature to you, not second nature.

Joy

Joy is from the Greek *#5479* in *Strong's Concordance.*

JOY: G5479 chara *khar-ah'* From G5463; *cheerfulness,* that is, calm *delight:* - gladness, X greatly, (X be exceeding) joy (-ful,-fully,-fulness,-ous).

ROOT WORD OF JOY: G5463 chairō *khah'ee-ro* A primary verb; to be full of *"cheer",* that is, calmly *happy* or well off; impersonal especially as a salutation (on meeting or parting), *be well:* - farewell, be glad, God speed, greeting, hail, joy (-fully), rejoice.

Joy is from the root *#5463,* which says "calmly happy or well off". It comes from a salutation meaning "be well". It is a greeting. The actual word that Paul is using, *#5479,* is cheerfulness, which means "calm delight". I suppose we always think of joy as being something exuberant.

Joy means calm delight.

Joy ought to be constant, not an occasional happening, as an outburst. We are not talking about something that happens; we are talking about a state of being. I am not talking about something we dress up in on Sunday mornings for an hour. I am not talking about something we dress up in when we meet someone, and we put on our self-righteous robes. I am talking about a state of being.

Do you think God is in a state of being? Then do you think we ought to be in a state of being with Him? Have you read the scripture that says,

29

28For in him we live, and move, and have our being...
Acts 17:28

"In Him we...have our being" means in Him you have your existence. What a shallow thing to be in Christ or be in the Father, and then you act like the devil. You can say that in Him we have our being, as if that were a safe place, but that safe place depends on the absence of sin. It is difficult for you to have fellowship with the Lord while you are in adultery.

In *Strong's* the Greek word *#5479* for joy, means gladness, then greatly, be exceedingly joyful, a fullness of joy. So it takes us from a state of being to an expression, but the expression should not be the beginning. It should be the extension. How many of you want to be joyful this year? The joy of the Lord is my strength.

10...for the joy of the LORD is your strength. Nehemiah 8:10

The kingdom of God is joy in the Holy Ghost.

17For the kingdom of God is not meat and drink; but righteousness, and peace, and joy in the Holy Ghost.
Romans 14:17

PEACE

Peace means to join. It is *Strong's #1515* in the Greek.

PEACE: G1515 eirēnē *i-rah'-nay*—Probably from a primary verb (to *join*); peace (literally or figuratively); by implication *prosperity:* - one, peace, quietness, rest, + set at one again.

Peace means "to join".
You cannot have peace if you are not joined

together with someone else.

When you are at differences with another person, you have no peace. When you are joined together, like-minded, you have peace together. When you do not have peace, you have strife. Scripture says,

> [16]For where envying and strife *is*, there *is* confusion and every evil work. James 3:16

So then where there is peace, there is every good thing.

I am committed to having peace with you. Will you have peace with me? The Bible says,

> [18]If it be possible, as much as lieth in you, live peaceably with all men. Romans 12:18

It does not say to live peaceably just with God, but live peaceably one with another. You cannot live peaceably with me when you say, "Well, I do not like you, Pastor". Then you are not joined to me.

Co-joined together is peace.

You're stuck with me. You might as well find your place of peace with me. I am stuck with you, and I might as well find my place of peace with you. Anything that comes in place of that peace has to go. Someone has to yield. Someone has to change. Someone has to let something go. Here, peace also means prosperity, quietness, rest, a place of quiet, belonging, being, state of being, and state of belonging.

Longsuffering

Longsuffering means long enduring. It is *Strong's* Greek word *#3115.*

LONGSUFFERING: G3115 makrothumia *mak-roth-oo-mee'-ah*   From the same as G3116; *longanimity,* that is, (objectively) *forbearance* or (subjectively) *fortitude:* - longsuffering, patience.

ROOT WORD OF LONGSUFFERING: G3116 makrothumós *mak-roth-oo-moce'*   Adverb of a compound of G3117 and G2372; with long (enduring) temper, that is, leniently: - patiently.

The root is from *#3116,* which means "with long enduring". Then it has a word called temper, long enduring temper. So the root of longsuffering is built into not losing your temper. When you lose your temper, you are not manifesting longsuffering. The root word for longsuffering also means being lenient. Lenient to me means putting up with other people's stuff* and patiently doing so. Now the actual word that is used by Paul, *#3115,* means forbearance, fortitude and patience. Longsuffering seems to indicate that there may be friction; otherwise you would not lose your temper. Wow. That is a hard one.

Gentleness

Gentleness means usefulness, excellence in character or demeanor, gentleness, kindness. It is *Strong's #5544* in the Greek and is from the root *#5543,* which means to be employed, useful in manner or morals. Gentleness, to me,

---

* Refer to Be in Health™ Idioms.

would be like having me serve you or having me employed by you for your benefit.

GENTLENESS: G5544 chrēstotēs   *khray-stot'-ace*   From G5543; *usefulness*, that is, moral *excellence* (in character or demeanor): - gentleness, good (-ness), kindness.

ROOT WORD OF GENTLENESS: G5543 chrēstos *khrase-tos'* From G5530; employed, that is, (by implication) useful (in manner or morals): - better, easy, good (-ness), gracious, kind.

ROOT OF THE ROOT: G5530 chraomai *khrah'-om-ahee* to furnish what is needed; (give an oracle, "graze" [touch slightly], light upon, etc.), that is, (by implication) to employ or (by extension) to act towards one in a given manner: - entreat, use.

This is a powerful insight because gentleness means "I defer to you". I am gentle with you because I defer to you, but in deferring to you, I am serving you.

Gentleness means
serving others for their benefit.

Most of us have never even considered the word "gentle" to even include anything like this. This is mind-bending at times because we always think gentleness is just being kind to someone. Are you being kind to them because you are condescending, or are you being kind to them because you are just trying to avoid them? Gentleness means you are deferring to them, serving them, as if you are employed by that person. Gentleness is deferring to them, serving them, undergirding them, and meeting them where they need you.

Goodness

Goodness means "goodness, which is a virtue" and is *Strong's Concordance #19* in the Greek. It comes from the root *#18,* which means "good".

GOODNESS: G19 agathōsunē ag-ath-o-soo'-nay— goodness, that is, virtue or beneficence: - goodness.

ROOT WORD OF GOODNESS: G18 agathos ag-ath-os' A primary word; "good" (in any sense, often as noun): - benefit, good (-s, things), well.

Is God filled with mercy? Yes.

7Blessed *are* the merciful: for they shall obtain mercy.

Matthew 5:7

You are filled with goodness when you manifest mercy to someone. When you are God-like in your contact with someone, you are filled with goodness. When you forgive someone, you are filled with goodness towards them because God also forgives. So to forgive others is to be God-like. **Goodness is the attribute of God's character in you which you give to others.** The definition, when you extend it, means "God-like".

Goodness means "God-like".

When you say, "the goodness of my heart," you are saying, "I have blessings for you. I have things that if I were God, I would give you". So, if you are giving all that you can give to a person, as if you were God, then you are God-like, and you are filled with charity and goodness. You are extending out to another from your goodness. If you grudgingly give, that is not goodness. That is being a Scrooge.

Goodness is giving the attributes
of God's character to others.

Faith

Faith means persuasion, credence, truthfulness and is #4102 in *Strong's*. Faith involves something that is credible. Do you think your faith should be based on credible things or incredible things? Faith is based on what is taught, in truth, as a statement of who God is and what He has said. Faith is believing the author of the statement.

FAITH: G4102 pistis *pis'-tis—* From G3982; *persuasion*, that is, *credence*; moral *conviction* (of *religious* truth, or the truthfulness of God or a religious teacher), especially *reliance* upon Christ for salvation; abstractly *constancy* in such profession; by extension the system of religious (Gospel) *truth* itself: - assurance, belief, believe, faith, fidelity.

ROOT WORD OF FAITH: G3982 peithō *pi'-tho* A primary verb; to *convince* (by argument, true or false); by analogy to *pacify* or *conciliate* (by other fair means); reflexively or passively to *assent* (to evidence or authority), to *rely* (by inward certainty): - agree, assure, believe, have confidence, be (wax) content, make friend, obey, persuade, trust, yield.

The root word is #3982, which means to convince as true or false, the authority, the confidence to obey, to persuade, to yield, to trust. How God thinks and what He has said are found when you read your Bible.

Romans 10:17 says,

[17]So then faith cometh by hearing, and hearing by the word of God.   Romans 10:17

35

Then you mix what God said with your faith, and you yourself now believe. If you believe what God said, that makes you a friend of God.

> **23And the scripture was fulfilled which saith, Abraham believed God, and it was imputed unto him for righteousness: and he was called the Friend of God.**
>
> James 2:23

Meekness

Meekness means humility and is *Strong's #4236.* It is from the root *#4235,* which means to be humble, gentle. You might say that meekness would cause you to prefer others above yourself. Moses was called the meekest of all men.

> **3(Now the man Moses *was* very meek, above all the men which *were* upon the face of the earth.)** Numbers 12:3

Meekness means not exalting yourself over another and taking into consideration the fact that you might be wrong.

MEEKNESS: G4236 praotēs *prah-ot'-ace* From G4235; *gentleness*; by implication *humility:* - meekness.

ROOT WORD OF MEEKNESS: G4235 praos *prah'-os* A form of G4239, used in certain parts; *gentle*, that is, *humble:* - meek.

ROOT OF THE ROOT: G4239 praus *prah-ooce'* Apparently a primary word; *mild*, that is, (by implication) *humble:* - meek.

TEMPERANCE

Temperance means self-control, continence and is *Strong's #1466.* It is your ability to say yes or no. Temperance is your ability to hold every thought in captivity. Temperance is your ability to choose good or evil. Temperance is tied into your will.

> TEMPERANCE: G1466 egkrateia *eng-krat'-i-ah* From G1468; *self control* (especially *continence*): - temperance.
>
> ROOT OF TEMPERANCE: G1468 egkratēs *eng-krat-ace'* From G1722 and G2904; *strong in* a thing (*masterful*), that is, (figuratively and reflexively) *self controlled* (in appetite, etc.): - temperate.
>
> ROOT OF THE ROOT: G2904 kratos *krat'-os* Perhaps a primary word; *vigor* ["great"], (literally or figuratively): - dominion, might [-ily], power, strength.

God is a God of self-control. God is a being who is true to His own words. Self-control involves being true to your own words. Temperance involves a decision that you should live and abide by and is based on how God thinks. If you cannot say anything good, do not say anything at all.

> **12But above all things, my brethren, swear not, neither by heaven, neither by the earth, neither by any other oath: but let your yea be yea; and *your* nay, nay; lest ye fall into condemnation.** James 5:12

You are either manifesting the kingdom of God or that other kingdom.

What God wants is for "who He is" to manifest through us as a way of life, moment by moment, hourly, daily, weekly, monthly, and yearly. I would encourage you to take this teaching and list these nine attributes of God's nature. Study these characteristics. Do not just get them into your head. Pray that they will get into your heart.

God Himself upholds all of creation by the Word of His power, and every word, every "jot and tittle" shall be performed and shall come to pass.

> ³Who being the brightness of his glory, and the express image of his person, and upholding all things by the word of his power, when he had by himself purged our sins, sat down on the right hand of the Majesty on high; Hebrews 1:3

As the snow falls, melts, returns, evaporates and falls back again as rain to the earth, to water the land, to bring forth the crops, so the Word of God is like that and shall accomplish that which it was sent to accomplish.

Maybe you will grow into all nine attributes by the end of a year. There are nine months to a school year, so maybe by the end of a school year you will have manifested these characteristics for most of the time.

To be like Him is my heart. Is it your heart to be like God? God saved you to change you into His image. What you lost because of sin, He wants to restore to you. I want you to be like God.

You will never be a god, and you will never be sinless this side of your glorification, but God wants you to begin to change. I want to be a peacemaker. I want to be a part of the solution, not the pollution. I want to be a living epistle, not a

SCUD missile*. I want to show up and be a gift to people. How many of you want to be a gift to people instead of a wrapped time bomb, ready to go off at a hair trigger? God really has called you to be a gift forever to mankind. That is what you will be as kings and priests, a gift to mankind.

As I close, I want to give you the <u>secret ingredient</u> to your preservation, if you will apply these principles. It is found in the latter part of Galatians 5:23, and it says, "Against such there is no law".

Against Such There Is No Law

Law is something that is enforced. God oversees His law to enforce it. Satan oversees his law to enforce it. When we do not follow the law of God, we yield ourselves to another law that is enforced by another spirit ruler, which is Satan and his kingdom. We come under the power of Satan. Paul talked about God's people being held captive by Satan at his will.

> **26And *that* they may recover themselves out of the snare of the devil, who are taken captive by him at his will.**
>
> 2 Timothy 2:26

**Believers can only be held captive
by Satan at his will
<u>if</u> they give themselves over to the law of Satan.**

Then we come under the law of sin, and it negates the benefits of the law of God. We need to know the truth so we can come to repentance and recover ourselves.

---

* Refer to Be In Health™ Idioms.

25In meekness instructing those that oppose themselves; if God peradventure will give them repentance to the acknowledging of the truth; 2 Timothy 2:25

Many of you will fall in some of these nine areas before you finish this day. Sunday mornings are war zones for the defeat of these characteristics of God. We should allow the Holy Spirit to be our guide, to teach us, convict us, and illuminate God's Word to us. In times of conflict when that other law is screaming in our heads, when our bodies are convulsing and the rage is on the end of our tongue, we should get lockjaw! Then when they look at you walking around your house with lockjaw, and they say, "What is your problem?" Then you say, "I am an overcomer".

23...against such there is no law. Galatians 5:23

You cannot be defeated if you are loving someone. You cannot be defeated if you have faith. You cannot be defeated if you have gentleness, goodness, and temperance. You cannot be defeated, and the promise of God is that He will defend you because you have become like Him.

God bless you.

BE IN HEALTH™ IDIOMS

Icky — Literally strange, funny substance. It means feeling out of sorts, like something is not right; a hunch, intuition, or sense of incorrectness.

Lay a heavy one on — Literally to hit you hard. It means a serious matter for consideration.

SCUD missile — Literally, in the Desert Storm war, a swiftly moving missile. The implied meaning is a person who defiles another.

Slurping — Literally, to drink something noisily. It means demonstrative affection without sincerity.

Sniffers — Literally, sniffing means to smell food before eating it. It implies new people coming to church to see if they like the church and the people; trying it.

Stuff — Literally, raw material from which anything is made. It means the part of our life that is not sanctified.

SCRIPTURE INDEX

- NOTES -